WAR HEROES AND OTHER OBSERVATIONS

THE BATTLES WE FIGHT EVERYDAY: A COLLECTION OF POEMS

MUKESH K SHARMA

Made with ♥ on the Notion Press Platform
www.notionpress.com

This book is dedicated to the cherished memory of **Bharat Bhushan**, a brother in spirit and heart, whose life and loving family were tragically taken by COVID-19. Their light continues to guide us through the words on these pages.

Contents

Contents

Contents

Preface

In the quiet moments of reflection, poetry often finds its breath, and within these pages, it seeks to echo the pulse of myriad lives altered by the ravages of war and the silent battles fought in the corridors of the everyday.

"War Heroes and Other Observations" is more than a collection of poems; it is a gathering of untold stories, whispered legacies, and unyielding courage. As an English lecturer, my days are steeped in the grand narratives of literature, where every tragedy and triumph is a lesson in the human saga. Yet, it is in the margins of these grand tales that I found the whispers that needed a voice—the tales of war heroes not clad in medals, but in the resilience of the human spirit.

This collection is my homage to those heroes and to the enduring human spirit that continues to aspire, love, and hope even in the most despairing of times. Each verse is a thread in the fabric of a narrative that belongs to all of us; they are observations of life's complexities and the quiet heroism that often goes unnoticed.

The impetus for this anthology is deeply personal. It is a tribute to my brother-like friend, Bharat Bhushan, whose life was a testament to the extraordinary courage found in ordinary existence. His untimely departure, along with his beloved family due to the COVID-19 pandemic, has left a void that words can scarcely fill. Yet, it is through these words that I seek to honor his memory and the countless others who have faced the unimaginable with dignity and grace.

To you, the reader, I present these poems as a mirror and a window—a reflection of the shared human experience and a glimpse into the lives that continue to inspire and move us. May you find within these lines a resonant truth, a comforting solace, and a renewed sense of kinship with the world around you.

Mukesh K. Sharma

Acknowledgements

No book is an island, and this collection of poems, least of all. It is the outcome of a confluence of many hearts, minds, and spirits, which have graciously poured into my life and, in turn, into these pages.

I am deeply grateful to my parents, whose unwavering faith in me has been the cornerstone of my resolve. They have instilled in me the love of words and the courage to express them. Their blessings have been my guiding light, shaping the person and the poet I am today.

To my beautiful wife, whose love and patience know no bounds, you are the quiet haven of support and the joyful muse to my creations. And to my beloved children, who remind me every day that the purest essence of observation is to see the world through the eyes of wonder and innocence—you are my daily inspiration.

I extend my heartfelt thanks to friends who have been the pillars of strength and wisdom—Dr. Garima Jain and Dr. Sona Agarwal, both Associate Professors with the Government of Rajasthan, whose insights and encouragements have been invaluable. Your friendship is a treasure I hold dear.

A special note of gratitude to my mentor, Dr. Devendra Singh, Associate Professor, University of Delhi, who has been a lighthouse in the foggy seas of my journey as a writer. Your mentorship has not only shaped my scholarly pursuits but has also emboldened my poetic voice.

To all those who have walked with me, in conversation, in silence, in the ebb and flow of life—thank you. This book reflects the richness that your presence has brought to my life.

Mukesh K. Sharma

1. homecoming

Lanterns paint the fractured streets,
Sparklers weave a web of shattered light.
A soldier walks where memory retreats,
Home a stranger in the crackling night.
His city wears this festival like bone,
The joy turned ash, a laughter turned to groan.
The rockets' echoes in his hollow mind
Mimic the thunder where his soul was left behind.
No lamps are lit to guide his stumbling form,
His heart, a fragment in the festive storm.
Familiar faces glow in gilded flame,
Each name a wisp of smoke he can't reclaim.
In broken temples, he lights a prayer so thin,
Not for safe return, but to atone for sin.
The whispered wish dissolves on blackened air:
To know this place again, this home he cannot bear.
Diwali's end won't wash away this stain,
He's but a shell now, where a man had once been slain.

2. underneath the uniform

Each alley gapes, a threat within the dark,
The weight of eyes she wills herself not to mark.
Footfalls echo hers, or do they mock her stride?
The uniform that should protect now makes her want to hide.
Her colleagues' voices boom, their casual jokes land wrong,
Each laugh a subtle echo of where she doesn't quite belong.
The radio, a hiss, the static amplifies her dread,
As if the very city whispers doubt within her head.
What if she falters, stumbles on the call?
Their silent judgment then, the cruellest blow of all.
The streets become a maze, every corner holds a doubt,
Each fleeting shadow makes her question what she's about.
The badge burns heavy, a beacon and a curse,
She doubts if strength exists beneath this worsening verse.
The siren's call now pierces her with fear,
Each night, a test she can't quite bring herself to clear.

3. foundations

Hands that shaped a life now shake and strain,
Against the mortar, each brick a weight unknown.
The mason's sharp eyes track his weakened frame,
And with each trembling heave, the old man's fear has grown.
Years carved in wrinkles, calluses deep and wide,
Tell tales of strength the body now denies.
He was a cornerstone, where walls took sturdy root,
Now clumsy feet betray him, pride a withered shoot.
He longs to toss the trowel, find a shadowed space,
But hunger gnaws, more brutal than disgrace.
Each coin clutched tight, a desperate, fading chime,
His worth now counted out in dwindling, borrowed time.
The houses rise, indifferent to his plea,
The mason's patience thinning, all too clear to see.
Soon, a younger pair of hands will claim this spot,
He reads the verdict on the wall, his purpose now forgot.

4. desert dreams

Where scorching sands meet endless, shifting skies,
The shepherd walks, with weathered dreams in eyes.
His flock, a cloud of dust against the sun,
While in his heart, another journey's spun.
No emerald fields, nor streams for him to claim,
His wealth, the stars that only darkness can inflame.
He yearns not for the palace, or for gold,
But simple justice, and a tale his bones can hold.
To see his lambs grow strong, the rains fall true,
To share a laugh with kin, with hearts born anew.
The city's distant shimmer holds no spell,
But honest trade, his wool to freely sell.
To raise his sons with head unbowed and proud,
His weathered voice no longer lost within the crowd.
The market's hum to ring with his name's worth,
To taste the fruit of labor, his own patch of earth.
And when the twilight comes, his journey done,
To leave a legacy his children carry on.
These are the treasures that the desert whispers low,
The shepherd's dream where worth, not wind, will blow.

5. to bharat bhushan

Ten days. A world collapsed, reduced to breath,
Husband, parents swallowed by that tide of death.
Their faces quiaflicker, ghost lights in her head,
Where echoes of their laughter mingle with the dead.
Two sons now cling, bewildered by their fears,
Their small hands reaching out through endless tears.
She wants to shield them, carve a space apart,
Yet grief has made a cavern of her heart.
The house, once warm, now whispers tales of loss,
With every passing hour, her pain a sharpened cross.
Their empty chairs, a silent, gaping cry,
And nights stretch long beneath a starless sky.
With each new dawn, she wills her feet to tread,
To be a mother, when her soul feels cold and dead.
The simple acts of living pierce her veil,
A world gone grey, where colors fail.
And through it all, guilt serpent-coils and stings,
Why was she spared, the one that sorrow wings?
Ten days of ash, a cruel and bitter span,
Now marked upon her with an unseen brand.

6. to a eunuch

The market stares, a thousand eyes unkind,
He shuffles past, his laughter long resigned.
A beggar's wage in this unyielding land,
The coins they offer sting his calloused hand.
His song, once meant for joy, now cracks and strains,
Its echoes mock him on these crowded lanes.
Cast out before his life could truly dim,
No temple holds a place for one like him.
At nights, a scrap of cloth beneath the moon,
He counts the coins, a hollow, soulless tune.
While longing for a home so far away,
Survival's cost, a price he pays each day.
The children point and whisper as he goes,
Their jeers a thorn on which his spirit grows.
Bearing a life both heavy and absurd,
A eunuch's heart, unseen, forever barred.

7. the cost

His desk, a lonely island in a sea of palms outstretched,
A lifetime's work built on the ink of honest ledgers kept.
Now names he dared not question rise like wraiths, tempest-blessed,
And accusations sting where once his duty found its rest.
Each file, once routine, now hisses with conspiracy,
Their signatures like fangs, a mockery of what should be.
The bribe he never took – a phantom coin his hands now hold –
Condemns him in this game where truth is bought and sold.
Sunlight filters through the blinds like prison bars he cannot break,
The room a stage where puppets dance, while honesty's at stake.
The higher powers loom, their laughter laced with cruel delight,
As shadows gather where a simple clerk once walked in light.
They'll twist his words, fabricate the ledger's honest line,
A sacrifice to appease the hunger of some dark, corrupt design.
And echoes of his pleas will fade, unheard, in marbled halls,
This honest clerk, another name that ruin's shadow calls.

8. paperwork

No time for gods now, in this sterile place,
Her prayer a scream caught in the fluorescent light.
Her child, a fading star, his tiny face
Lost against the endless paperwork they cite.
Rules etched in ink, more precious than a breath,
While time leaks out, a crimson thread undone.
Her husband's ghost beside her, cold as death –
Their world collapses, life and laughter gone.
What worth is bureaucracy, cold and neat,
Against the wild despair she knows too well?
Two years of joy, now scattered at her feet,
The forms they offer mock her private hell.
Her son slips under, carried by the tide,
While ink dries slow, and hearts turn stark and wide.

9. war heroes

First they create war; a fevered, hungry beast,
Its siren call of glory weaves a fatal thread.
And they create war heroes, plucked from fields of feast,
To feed the hungry maw while those in power spread.
Their names like anthems on the mourning breeze,
Yet built on whispers, on unhallowed ground.
For what is valor when those victories
Serve puppet masters hidden, never crowned?
"First they create war; and they create war heroes,"
The bitter verse a dirge of shattered bone.
Who weeps for truth with every flag that billows,
When victors dance on ash, and blood alone?
Let this line echo as the battle hymn expires,
Exposing architects bathed in shadowed fires.

10. the bargain

The market buzzes, gold, and silks like sin.
He shrinks inside, where shame has carved its place.
Their eyes, like scales, weigh value he can't win,
Each bangle on her wrist, a nail upon his face.
His laughter died the day that bargain struck,
His daughter's smile a moon on borrowed light.
To be a father now fills him with such dread,
Each rupee begged cuts deeper in the night.
Tradition strangles like a gilded rope,
And hollowed pride whispers a desperate plan.
His debt, a serpent coiling in his hope,
The groom a specter, not her cherished man.
The wedding looms, a pyre to joy unbuilt,
His daughter's fate, a dowry yet unfilled.

11. death-certificate

The clerk's dull eyes, two pennies on a grave,
Flicker in the fluorescent wasteland of this hall.
His father is a smudge on paper, lost in waves
Of faceless files, their silence like a pall.
Third time he treads this maze of stamped decay,
Where time turns rubber, each official face a stone.
Hope is a tattered form that fades away,
Meaning whispers lost in every unanswered phone.
His father's life, reduced to queue and date,
Mocks the grief held taut within his chest.
The wheels of office grind him into fate,
While echoes of a burial find no rest.
Lost in forms, and dates no tears redeem,
His father's death certificate, still a haunting dream.

12. the loan

Dust whispers parched prayers where furrows lie,
The empty well reflects a vacant sky.
Calloused hands twist, not in work but need,
He counts not harvest now, but barren seed.
The banker sits where no rain ever falls,
His columns stark against the pleading calls.
The ledger's ink turns red against his name,
Each promised bushel now a mark of shame.
No April rains to swell the sunbaked ground,
Only debt's harsh echo, a relentless sound.
He sees his children's eyes, wide with silent blight,
Their hunger carves a debt no coins can right.
His land, a parchment scrawled with fading green,
Where once was plenty, now the cracks are seen.
This borrowed soil he's tilled with sweat and bone,
Feels alien now, as cold as weathered stone.
The city towers mock with sterile gleam,
Their lights devour his fading, dirt-worn dream.
He turns away, from promise turned to dust,
Another season gone, and broken trust.

13. the prisoner

The classroom holds a feathered ghost,
Pigeon wings like panicked smoke,
Against cold glass, a futile boast,
The sunlight but a winter joke.
Where desks lie bare, once children roared,
This creature claws a phantom sky.
No open field, no flock to hoard,
The vacant room, its lonely cry.
Eyes like beads, black seeds of fear,
Each beat of wings, a brutal prayer.
Hunger gnaws, the world grows drear,
A captive of the frosty air.
Stone heart of school, this empty place,
Yet life persists, leaves desperate trace.
The pigeon's dance, a savage grace,
Against the chill, it finds no space.

14. first stand

Spindle legs like brittle sticks,
Hooves splayed wide, unsure and slick.
The earth a sea, the body sways,
Blind eyes blink in the barn's dim haze.
Muscles ripple, a jolt, a strain,
The scent of straw and mother's mane.
Each stumble burns with a newborn plea –
The world unfurling, so vast to see.
A wobble, a twitch, the haunches rise,
The head held high, a lowing cries.
To taste the air, defy the fall,
Against the vastness, stand so small.
Every tremor a battle won,
A life ignited with morning sun.
In awkward triumph, legs untried,
The world awaits, stretched open wide.

15. the orphan

Eyes the color of weathered stones,
Carrying burdens far beyond their bones.
Tiny hands, with lines too deep,
Selling trinkets while the city sleeps.
Sunken stomach, a silent plea,
For kindness lost, a family.
Yet, a flicker in that young heart's flame,
A spirit wild, untamed by shame.
Each coin earned, a victory cry,
Against the odds that soar so high.
For in the dust, a flower yearns,
Where strength in fragile petals burns.
The eyes may hold a world of tears,
But in the soul, a hope appears.
Like stars that pierce the darkest night,
An orphan's dream, a guiding light.
For kindness lives in unseen ways,
And with each dawn, a brighter phase.
The heart that bleeds, can still believe,
In whispered songs the soul will weave.

16. a car wash

A film of grime, a world so gray,
The ceaseless drone of engines all the day.
He coughs, a rattle in his burdened chest,
The city's breath upon him, never at rest.
Suds and spray, the endless turn,
Of gleaming paint where old dreams burn.
No children's laughter fills his empty years,
Only the echo of unspoken fears.
The endless avenues, a fractured maze,
Reflect the weariness of endless days.
He scrubs and buffs, a figure worn and slight,
Lost within this urban, fading light.
And as the dusk descends in somber streaks,
Of fleeting wealth and power he never seeks,
A single streetlamp casts a mournful beam –
A life unraveled, adrift within a dream.

17. furnace eyes

Glass shards dance in molten glow,
Where futures bend, sight begins to go.
A cough ignites the furnace air,
Each fiery bangle hangs suspended there.
Thin wrists adorned, where his hands betray,
The hollow glitter of a fading day.
Colors swirl, a fractured light,
Green and purple, in approaching night.
He molds the heat with weakened touch,
Dreams once shimmering, now mean so much.
The kiln, his altar, sweat his holy dew,
Where sight dissolves, and forms break anew.
The final twist, a fading craftsman's art,
Mirrors the blindness creeping on his heart.

18. an expensive education

Rote words whispered, ancient text unknown,
Sunlight barred, where youthful minds are sown.
The measured cadence of a faith defined,
Seeking answers that remain confined.
His gaze drifts past the window's shadowed square,
To unseen worlds he cannot truly share.
The hum of verses, an endless, pulsing plea,
For truths untouched, a knowledge yet to be.
Each sacred verse, a double-edged design,
Comfort found, yet broader thought may decline.
He traces letters, histories swept away,
Where science sleeps, and questions dare not stay.
The world outside, a blur of vibrant sound,
Fades against the doctrine's hallowed ground.
A scholar forged, or spirit left untamed?
Within these walls, his destiny unnamed.

19. quietude

The house, it echoes now, a shell
Where laughter danced, and small feet fell.
Each room, a ghost of what once was,
The vibrant hum now gentle hush.
Toys gathered dust in lonely rows,
Bedrooms vacant where childhood once flowed.
The scent of warm meals, a fading thing,
Dinner table whispers no longer will ring.
A bittersweet wind chills the space,
Time paints wrinkles on a mother's worn face.
Where are those hands she used to hold,
Nurtured wings now flown, stories untold.
The nest built with love, now bare and stark,
The heart a strange mix, heavy and light as a lark.
Did life rush too swiftly, was it all fleeting grace?
The empty rooms call for a redefined space.
Yet with the quiet, a strange freedom unfurls,
No battles or schedules, a forgotten world.
Sleep stretches leisurely, once snatched and so small,
A self rediscovered, emerging and tall.
No longer just "mother", but the woman beneath,
With passions forgotten, to once more re-breathe.
This aching hollow, a space held with care,

For dreams once deferred, new chapters to dare.
The empty nest echoes, a bittersweet theme,
Yet love lingers on, though altered its gleam.
It's time to fly solo, with heart strangely light,
Embracing the sunset, on this soft, gentle night.

20. lighthouse

Old bones I stand, by salt winds worn,
Witness to sea tales, since time was born.
Seagulls my courtiers, restless and white,
I stand here steadfast, day bleeding to night.
Ships rise on swells, figures etched small,
Men braced for weather, to rise or to fall.
I've seen the kraken in hungry storms swell,
Brave spirits swallowed, the sea a dark well.
Fishermen cast nets, small prayers unfurled,
Eyes etched with stories of this watery world.
They come and they vanish, with tides ebb and flow,
While my lonely light paints the darkness below.
And lovers too, drawn to the ocean's cold heart,
Promise and whisper where land falls apart.
How fragile their vessels, how brief their warm flame,
Lost whispers devoured by tides without name.
Yet still I stand tall, with my sentinel grace,
My beam slicing fog, chasing shadows apace.
For I know when men falter, hearts torn by the squall,
A beacon shines strongest when hope feels so small.
They trust in my promise, though battered and tossed,
Through the sea's darkest moments, when starlight is lost,
They know from the distance, their safe voyage waits,

And I guide them towards harbor, past ocean's dark gates.
I am weathered and ancient, my stone heart holds tight,
All the secrets of sailors, by day and by night.
A metaphor, whispered, though I utter no sound,
Lighthouse and life, on this storm-driven ground.

21. caged

They flicker at the edges of my days,
Whispers of paths untaken, untrodden ways.
A painter's hand stilled, replaced by a file,
The dancer's forgotten music, her step gone a while.
In quiet hours, when work becomes haze,
They rise, these forgotten dreams, in ghostly ballet.
The writer in me, stories trapped like caged birds,
Imagined novels dissolving to practical words.
I see them reflected in eyes worn and wise,
Of friends bound by duty, the dimming light in their eyes.
Whispers of singers on stages untamed,
Or astronauts yearning where starlight still flamed.
We chose stability, roof, and safe bread,
Yet something within us softly mourned as we tread.
Did we miss our true North, in the hustle and scheme?
The cost of survival – extinguishing dreams.
There's no grand lament, no tears for the lost,
Just a gnawing sensation, the price that we crossed.
We bury desires in the cracks of routine,
Yet shadows still dance where 'could have been' gleams.
Maybe in stolen moments, a verse might break free,
A stolen brushstroke, or a dance held secretly.
Those flickering spectres that walk by our side

Show the lives trapped within, we so carefully hide.
Forgotten dreams, not vanquished but sleeping,
Whispering softly, their slow vigil keeping.
Perhaps within twilight, with courage untold,
We'll find a sliver of what made our hearts bold.

22. exodus

They left with sunbaked dreams on bundled backs,
Eyes tracing roads that offered no looking back.
Small villages dissolving with each restless tread,
Rumors of cities where hunger is fed.
Promises shimmered on concrete and glass,
Whispering sweet lies where green fields surpassed.
Roots severed from loam, from ancestral decree,
The heart seeks its fortune on a restless, wide sea.
Cramped corners echo where fields once were wide,
The song of the oxen replaced by harsh tide.
Hands meant for harvest now peddle and pawn,
Small gods abandoned, new struggles at dawn.
The elders grow hollow, old wisdom turns stale,
Children forget songs woven for their birth vale.
A language dies softly, lost on factory floors,
Where community drowns in mechanical roars.
And nights ring with longing, a moon far too white,
Where city stars offer counterfeit light.
For what have they bartered, this trade of the known,
To stand rootless amidst crowds, aching alone?
Yes, some hands find coin, build small fragile rooms,
A roof may rise steady where uncertainty looms.
Yet, with each new triumph, a whisper so slight,

Of forgotten belonging, dreams strangled in flight.
Exodus of millions, the great urban swell,
Where promises crackle, both heaven and hell.
Progress, they call it, yet hearts mourn still
That space where a soul knew which place it could fill.

23. the watcher

On sill I perch, eyes like amber aglow,
Watcher unseen where human stories flow.
Through cracked blinds, I spy their secret domain,
Their mundane sorrows, and small whispered gains.
There's the woman who weeps by a flickering screen,
Lost loves and regrets in its pale bluish sheen.
A child at his desk, lost in a world made of words,
While parents wage war with glances like swords.
Old man by the fire, hands folded in sleep,
Dreams paint his face, with memories they keep.
And a girl by the mirror, twirling bright as a bird,
Before womanhood comes, with whispers unheard.
These lives I hold close, though no words pass between,
The weight of a heartbeat in each trembling scene.
A spilt cup of tea, a sigh unconfined,
These unnoticed moments where truth lies enshrined.
On rooftops I roam, in shadows I hide,
Watching their world like an unshifting tide.
Perhaps there's a lesson in all that I see,
Of joy unobserved, a fragile sweet plea.
That within the most ordinary, grand tales abide,
Of hopes and frail losses where spirits collide.
Though a stray at the window, my vigil takes flight,

In the silence and shadows, where lives find their light.

24. a tree

My roots grip earth, time-weathered and deep,
While seasons unfurl around me, in cycles they keep.
Children once carved their sweet vows in my side,
Lovers entwined where my branches provide.
I've stood sentinel here, as the town sprouted round,
My leaves drank of sun, roots firm in the ground.
Birdsong was symphony, wind my lone prayer,
Unbothered by progress, this space I did share
But now metal teeth growl, their hunger unknown,
The sweet scent of sawdust hangs stark in the morn.
The cries of the birds a dissonant plea,
As giants replace what was sacred to me.
Generations I've marked, cradled with shade,
Their battles and laughter beneath me were played.
Now concrete will creep where green tendrils unfurled,
They barter my heartbeat for their sterile new world.
I hear distant protests, murmurs too slight,
To drown out the clamor, the machinery's might.
A child's single teardrop falls hot on my bark,
But they cannot conceive this loss in the dark.
With one final groan, my reign takes its end,
In this cityscape stark, no space to extend.
I become timber, a table, a door,

My soul silenced forever, where wild roots did soar.
Perhaps in carved wood, some memory might bloom,
A last sigh of nature in a well-ordered room.
But mostly I fade, an echoing plea,
For those who will follow, when all the trees flee.

25. a letter unsent

The paper crinkles beneath my restless touch,
Ink stains like teardrops where emotions fight much.
Words struggle to bloom, form hesitant lines,
Confessions that festered through withering time.
Was it pride then, or fear, that stayed my warm hand?
To speak of the love I harbored like sand?
Should I have surrendered, laid bare my torn soul,
Risked scorn or indifference, to make myself whole?
Perhaps they would've laughed, called my feelings too bold,
And the warmth may have fled, leaving ashes too cold.
Or maybe their eyes would have softened in kind,
Mirrors reflecting the heart left behind.
Now time casts its shadow, the moment now lost,
Words wither unopened, their cost etched in frost.
The letter unfinished, a monument still,
To chances unguarded, a hope turned so chill.
Fingers now hover, not over the page,
But the weight of what's missing, the words trapped like rage.
Would it serve purpose, this ghost from the past,
Or open up wounds that a lifetime won't cast?
This unwritten echo I'll tuck close unseen,
A testament whispered, of all that could've been.
My unmailed confession, a love song so faint,

The music of longing, a bittersweet taint.
And so, with a sigh, it joins others untold,
In a box in my heart, where secrets grow old.
The last letter written, but never sent free,
A haunting reminder of all that won't be.

26. the keeper of lives

I stand with walls like weathered skin,
Each crack and dent a tale held within.
If tongues could unfurl from faded paint,
Oh, the songs they would sing, soft and faint.
A child's first wobbly step, imprinted bold,
Now echoes faintly as echoes grow old.
Laughter once rippled, like raindrops so bright,
But hushed now in stillness, like whispers of night.
Lovers murmured secrets, promises sweet,
Their warmth held captive in plaster and sheet.
Words angry and sharp hung heavy with sting,
The walls still remember, though long ceased to ring.
A lone plate abandoned, a half-finished tea,
Whispers of moments left hastily.
Photos hold smiles of a time swiftly flown,
While dust now descends where joy once was known.
And I, ever witness, silent and grand,
Cradle these echoes from hand to warm hand.
A piano untouched, its melody gone,
Leaving room for the wind to carry its song.
The heartbeats and tears, all absorbed in my grain,
A symphony fading, a bittersweet strain.
When inhabitants vanish, new echoes take hold,

But my memory dances, stories untold.
For I am the keeper of lives fleeting by,
Of sorrow and laughter beneath a wide sky.
These empty rooms whisper, my voice soft and low,
An echoing heartbeat of all I once known.

27. beyond broken straps

His hands, a testament to years of work,
each line and wrinkle carved by leather and thread.
His worn wooden bench his kingdom,
where tired shoes breathe a second life.
He sees beyond broken straps and gaping soles,
each scuff a chapter in a life well-worn.
The dancer's slippers, their graceful spins now faded,
the worker's boots bearing witness to cobbled streets.
A child's sandals, buckles straining from boundless energy,
hold stories of exploration and skinned knees.
He finds a tear-stained heel, a testament to heartbreak,
and works meticulously through the night.
With each deliberate stitch, he offers silent solace,
mending not just footwear, but spirits made weary.
His labor transcends the practical,
restoring the resilience woven into every step.
The cobbler knows each repaired journey speaks
of perseverance, and the ability to rise from hardship.
Under the soft glow of his lamp, amidst the scent of leather,
he pieces together fragments of lives,
offering silent testament to the strength inherent in us all.

28. the last empty leaf

The weight of a final line settles upon me,
a lifetime captured in hurried strokes.
Dreams shimmered here, some extinguished, others faintly glowing.
Loves unfolded, petals now dried and pressed between my fibers.
Wars were waged within these margins, small triumphs inked as battle scars.
Did the soul scribbling upon me leave a lasting mark?
Or will these words disappear, unnoticed whispers blown with the dust?
In my younger years, victories burned bright, but regrets are bolder now.
So many paths untrodden, chances let slip in moments of fear.
Yet, there was grace too, quiet acts of kindness etched in a trembling hand.
This is my worn legacy, the sum of a life in fading ink.
No chance to change the tale, nor rewind the relentless clock.
Soon, this weathered cover will fold shut, the story done.
I carry a final farewell, and slip into the silence between words.

29. the loom

I am the ancient loom, timeworn and wise,
each thread spun through me a fragile life.
With deft hands, I guide the warp and weft,
patterns emerging, where destinies are left.
A newborn's cry, a new strand woven bright,
sparkling and unblemished in the soft morning light.
Youth's vibrant hues dance boldly in the weave,
unaware of the fleeting years they must leave.
Threads mingle and cross, forming tangled designs,
loves entwined, hearts bound by invisible lines.
Some strands glow with fortune, a glittering prize,
while others wear thin, the brightness dimming from eyes.
There are threads cut too short, a promise denied,
leaving ragged gaps where a spirit once thrived.
And hues dimmed by grief, the pattern stained deep,
the shuttle falls silent, leaving loved ones to weep.
With each new strand taken, a tapestry unfolds,
stories of mortals in threads spun like gold.
Am I the master, crafting this grand fate,
or just a witness, as lives rise and abate?
Yet, there's beauty in chaos, in patterns untamed,
a testament to souls on life's journey proclaimed.
Though the ending is written, the story unknown,

I weave on with purpose, where destinities are sown.

30. the street violin

The worn cobblestones have borne witness to my song,
to laughter and tears drawn out by music so long.
My makeshift stage, a faded patch of concrete and light,
where I've bared my soul under star-studded night.
There's the old woman who sways to long-forgotten tunes,
eyes closed as her youth flickers back like new blooms.
A child leaves a coin, eyes as wide as the sky,
the first flicker of magic where dreams softly fly.
Lovers hold hands, their secret smiles caught in my refrain,
as melodies wash over their budding joy and sweet pain.
The worn traveler pauses, with burdens untold,
finding a moment of respite in tales spun of old.
A tapestry of faces, etched into my wandering heart,
yet their names like wisps of smoke, they quickly depart.
A fleeting audience captured by melodies sweet,
then carried away by the ever-turning, restless street.
Soon my violin case will lie empty and bare,
my voice just an echo lingering in the bustling square.
And the city will rumble, unchanged and unmoved,
a testament to those here momentarily loved.
The wind carries my farewell, a bittersweet sting,
a street performer's song is a transient, wild thing.
A connection in music, a moment held tight,

before I vanish once more into the restless night.

31. a statue in the park

Stone eyes gaze out, weathered and unyielding,
a silent witness to seasons endlessly revealing.
The world flows around me, a ceaseless, hurried beat,
while my vigil remains on this worn, familiar seat.
Lovers carve their vows in the trees at my feet,
words fading through seasons, promises bittersweet.
Their laughter mingles with the calls of nesting birds,
a symphony of living – fleeting, joyous words.
Children scurry past, chasing laughter and leaves,
unaware of the tales in the patterns time weaves.
They see merely stone, a backdrop to their play,
while I silently gather the stories of each passing day.
An old woman sits weeping, memories her shroud,
whispers blending with rustling leaves, barely allowed.
A businessman rushes, eyes lost in a screen's cold gleam,
missing the dappled sunlight that paints an ephemeral dream.
I absorb their dramas, their triumphs and despair,
each fleeting expression leaving a mark in the air.
Though my tongue is silent, my form still speaks so bold,
bearer of truths forgotten, memories grown old.
Perhaps in the stillness, where time seems to bend,
they'll sense my presence, their silent, stoic friend.

A reminder in stone, a guardian at rest,
that beneath the surface, there's more than eyes attest.

32. the teaching Business

Chalk dust chokes the air, yeah, like some ancient curse,
While they stare at glowing boxes, plugged into the universe.
Who wants Homer, Whitman, hell, who needs to read,
When viral fame's the drug, and empty likes they feed.
Forms and funds and rules that make me wanna puke,
They cut budgets, steal our spirit, break us on the hook.
Shoulda' been a poet, or a rock star with a scream,
Not this treadmill grind, killin' every damn dream.
But wait, a hand goes up, a question cuts the haze,
Some kid who ain't brain-dead, lost in the social maze.
They wanna know the why, the how, the hidden scheme,
And goddamn, for a second, maybe there's still a gleam.
Maybe this ain't a prison, or just a soul-dead waste,
Maybe one kid breaks the mold, finds that hunger, tastes
The words, the ideas, that crack the world apart,
Rebuild it from the wreckage, ignite that hungry heart.
So yeah, I teach, I fight, against the odds I scream,
'Cause that one kid, that question, keeps this weird job a dream.
The system sucks, the money's crap, the world's gone kinda mad,
But screw it, in this classroom, it's the best fight I ever had.

33. a night shift nurse

The world sleeps, or parties while I punch the clock,
Trading dreams for scrubs, in this fluorescent block.
The halls are shadowed whispers, beeping machines my song,
Where life plays out in moans, where strength battles the long...
And the long nights drag, caffeine ain't no match,
Blurred between a savior and a body parts dispatch.
I bandage fading starlight bleeding through the blinds,
And hold back secrets darker than these antiseptic lines.
Someone weeps for home, another prays for dawn,
I count the ceiling tiles till both of them are gone.
They see an angel or a robot, with my plastered-perfect smile,
Not this aching girl counting her own breaths to survive the mile.
Bills back home unopened, lover sleeps alone,
While I wipe a stranger's sweat, whisper "you're not thrown
Into this dark alone, hold on, just hold the hell on tight"
But damn, sometimes at daybreak, even I question the light.
Yet something drags me back, that flicker in their eye,
When my tired hands bring strength, when sobs finally go dry.
Not God, not glory – some messed up sense of right,
To be a rebel witness in this upside-down twilight.

So yeah, another graveyard shift, another dawn so near,
The pay sucks, hours brutal, but the battles...they feel clear.
This is my weird trench warfare, and when the sun ascends,
I walk outta here beaten, but goddamn, the world depends.

34. coal miners

Down we plunge, like sinners into hell,
Where sunlight is a myth old timers tell.
The earth above, a muffled symphony,
Replaced by dust and echoes haunting me.
Pick and shovel, my symphony of sweat,
The blackness clings, a suffocating debt.
Cages rise and fall, each ton a stolen heart,
From the mountain's wounded chest, we tear her all apart.
They talk of progress, warmth that lights the night,
But never see the shadows where we wage this fight.
Lungs fill with darkness, coughing up our years,
Each breath a whispered curse the world never hears.
Some call it honest work, a backbone to this land,
My aching joints tell stories they can't understand.
We fuel their world, unseen 'neath blackened skin,
Phantoms in the mines, where daylight dares not win.
Yet, there's a stubborn fire deep within my soul,
Kindled in the blackness by the glint of stolen coal.
The kinship forged in shadows, stronger than the sun,
When brothers haul each other out, the shift finally done.
Home ain't some picket fence, it's where the beer tastes cold,
A wife's worn hands, a story yet untold.
We live on borrowed time, each sunrise feels like theft,

But in the belly of the beast, strength is all we have left.
So yeah, we dig, we bleed, for progress and for pay,
But they ain't seein' ghosts walkin' in the light of day.
Maybe when the last seam's dry, the mountain left to weep,
The world will hear the echoes while we finally sleep.

35. the fisherman's last cast

Sun bleeds into the water,
makes the old sea blush
with shame maybe,
remembering days
when it foamed with life,
not this oily sheen
and plastic guts
spilled from factory ships.
The old man's net hangs loose,
like his weathered skin,
more holes than hope these days.
He's seen the catch dwindle,
the big ones turned to ghost stories,
their scales swapped for price tags
at some fancy fishmonger's stall.
His boat rocks, a cradle
for a dying lullaby.
Each creak echoes generations
who pulled sustenance from these waves,
before progress came
with diesel engines
and yawning nets that never tire.

They call it overfishing,
got some fancy chart or graph
to prove it,
but him, he sees
the greed reflected
in the gulls squawking
over scraps.
This last cast, it ain't about dinner,
hell, he hardly trusts what
might drag up with it,
some glowing mutant thing.
No, it's about spit in the eye
of progress, a small defiance,
a middle finger to the fat cats
getting richer while the ocean starves.
Maybe he pulls up nothing,
maybe a goddamn boot,
doesn't matter.
He's part of the poem of this place,
and when he's gone,
another verse gets erased,
and the whole damn song
falls flat.

36. the baker's dawn

Stars still clinging to the sky,
not like that fake city glow,
but real pinpricks in a fading velvet drape,
as flour dust motes catch the first weak light.
Old wooden floor creaks its morning song,
in tune with the baker's weary bones,
but ovens yawn hot and hungry,
and hands remember what feet still question.
Yeast and water sigh awake,
little lives blooming in the battered bowl,
the first promise of another day's sustenance.
He punches down dreams alongside the dough,
Kneads worries into twists and braids,
whispering secret hopes into rising loaves.
The radio crackles an old tune,
off-key singing fills the empty shop front.
Outside, the world still slumbers,
oblivious to this symphony of steam and sweat.
They'll smell the magic later, that warm bread scent,
and never guess the small miracles born each night.
He's not a hero, not in their stories,
with shiny capes or sirens in the street.
Just a man who greets the dawn with floured hands,

offering up his warmth, one golden loaf at a time.

37. the street vendor's symphony

Concrete jungle pulse is his metronome,
car horns and shouted curses
accompany his calloused sales pitch.
Wares spread on stained pavement,
knock-off dreams and plastic necessities,
glimmer faintly 'neath indifferent streetlights.
Faces flow by, a nameless tide,
some glance with suspicion, others blind as stone.
He's a blip on their radar, a hawker
blocking precious sidewalk space,
not the aching back, the child's empty plate,
tugging at him from back-alley shadows.
The city coughs diesel as buses rumble past,
suit-clad businessmen scowl over spilled coffee –
their worries weigh less than his unsold stock.
But then, a kid lingers, eyes bright with longing,
clutching a wrinkled dollar bill.
A battered toy changes hands, a smile breaks wide,
and for a heartbeat, the symphony shifts.
The vendor stands taller, city ain't so merciless,
not when he's spun a bit of magic from nothing,
one tiny transaction of survival

in the heart of this uncaring machine.

38. the rooftop gardener

Pigeons squabble over scraps below,
but up here, a different war takes root.
Hands stained with city grime coax blooms
from soil hauled up by creaking stairs.
Tarpaper rooftop bakes relentless,
while tomato vines wage slow battle,
zucchini sprawls with defiance,
peppers hold tiny fires against the sun.
The skyline ain't no painted masterpiece,
just water towers and office blocks,
but in this riot of mismatched pots,
the gardener sculpts their private rebellion.
No birdsong here, just distant subway whine,
but buzzing bees find forgotten sweetness,
prove life persists in asphalt cracks.
It ain't no farm, no idyllic meadow dream,
But under calloused hands,
a defiant harvest bursts to life.
Radish, a ruby miracle.
Chives, green defiance against gray.
Proof that something wild still yearns,
And up on this windblown, sun-beaten perch,
that yearning's enough to grow a tiny forest,

one defiant rooftop sprout at a time.

39. the taxi driver

Yellow blur in the stream-flow of traffic, metal beast weaving
concrete veins, the meter my heartbeat, ticking by fares,
by landmarks blurred like memories fading –
(Woman cries in the backseat, broken words like cracked
windows, leaking some lover's betrayal into stale vinyl)
Suitcase dreams bouncing in the trunk, airport bound, a leap
into flight, some city lights swapped for others –
(Laughter bursts like startled pigeons – kids sharing sticky
candy
smiles, the world small and sweet on cracked leather
upholstery)
The city speaks a dialect of exhaust, horns cursing in code,
my cab a confession booth on wheels, I bear witness
(Lost in translation, new arrival asks my help, the map of his
future crinkled with fear and a hope older than my worn
tires)
Headlights cut through fog, my own dreams smoke trails
blurring
at daybreak, shift done, I crawl back to a honeycomb cell of
sleep
(Meter resets to zero, miles devoured, leaving stories like
loose change

scattered on asphalt, waiting for some other wheel to crush them)
The city breathes me in, then out. Just another cog, one fare bleeding
into the next, an atlas of humanity printed on my soul,
each block, each mile, a line in this never-ending poem.

40. the conquered

Smoke-choked world, where walls collapse into teeth,
and he stands, a battered figure against the blaze.
The hose thrashes in his grip, a water-born serpent,
spewing its defiance at the fire's hungry mouth.
Each roar of the inferno is a challenge unfurled,
a battle in a realm of cinder and ember,
where men forge themselves in the belly of the beast,
ash-painted warriors tested by molten fury.
Flame licks and hisses, a taunting symphony,
but in its crucible, a different strength takes form.
Each blistering second tempers resolve,
builds scars into shields, fear into focus.
They call him hero, savior, words too pale,
They don't understand the dance with destruction,
the intimate knowledge of how quickly lives unravel,
how swiftly courage flickers and finds its fuel.
Fire consumes, a force primeval, untamed,
And yet, in his veins, a kindred burn persists.
He wrestles back the chaos, beat by beat,
taming the blaze, shaping the aftermath.
When sirens finally fade, and embers cease to glow,
a different echo lingers, a silent testament.
For in the ashes, he is both conqueror and conquered,

forged by fire, his spirit reflecting its restless light.

41. chai wala

Steam was his symphony, rising in fragrant spirals,
each hiss and bubble a song of sustenance.
Hands danced in ritual, chai masala his sacred spice,
the battered kettle his humble altar to the street.
Faces thronged his stall, dawn to dusk, seeking solace,
a pause in the city's ceaseless thrum. Sweet warmth
bloomed in chipped clay cups, gossip and laughter
the unwritten recipe passed down through generations.
Then silence fell, like an unseen shroud. The lockdown
caged him within walls too small for worry to breathe.
Each unsold cup a hollow promise, children's eyes
mirroring the dwindling flame of his kerosene stove.
The spice rack mocks him, vibrant dust now inert,
a cruel taunt against hunger's relentless gnaw.
The streets lie mute, his familiar call swallowed
by an indifferent pandemic sweeping hopes aside.
He dreams not of wealth, but the burnished glow
of his kettle, the chatter of those returning parched.
Each empty dawn, a battle of resilience, whispered
against the echoes of bustling mornings lost.
His hands, once sure in their craft, now ache
with the weight of an uncertain future. Yet,
beneath the despair, a defiant flame flickers –

the spirit of the chai wala, ready to brew life anew.

42. resident doctor

Scrubs his second skin, slept in more than lived in,
the gurney-wheeled world his never-ending shift.
Eyes burning with disinfectant-dawn light,
he charts survival not by hours, but by moans.
Home ain't no warm bed anymore,
just faces on a cracked cell phone screen,
voices fading to static with the 4 AM bleeps.
They talk of heroes on the nightly news,
Don't see the bags under bloodshot eyes,
The tremor in the hand that scribbles meds,
The coffee, cold and bitter, fueling this war
nobody signed up for, but gotta fight anyway.
Maybe if this was bombs, if the enemy screamed louder,
They'd give him a damn parade or at least a decent meal.
But the virus mocks flags and anthems,
and heroes bleed invisible in fluorescent hallways.
The seventh day? Just another white blur,
same coughs, same pleas, same silent oath
to patch this broken world one exhausted heartbeat at a time,
'cause that's what it means, even without applause.

43. the tourist

Camera slung like a plastic badge of conquest,
he maps the city with guidebook stares,
snapping selfies against weathered, unseen walls.
Beggars blend into the backdrop, just another local charm.
His designer sneakers tread paths worn
by generations seeking bread, not photo ops.
The market's shouts fade to white noise
beneath his curated playlist of escape.
Each sip of overpriced latte fuels the delusion
that he's tasting the "authentic", untouched.
While children hawk postcards their fathers drew,
he frames another panoramic lie for social feeds.
His guidebook boasts of history, of vibrant culture,
missing the hunger in hungry eyes, the pulse beneath the
posed smiles.
When he leaves, nothing shifts,
But somewhere a flicker of disdain stirs,
in those rendered invisible by his well-intentioned gaze.

44. progress

Where the corner store once stood, its awning faded,
Now towers a monolith of glass and slick veneer.
Neon promises deals the old sign never dared,
whispering of lattes, of lives upgraded here.
Old Mr. Singh swept that sidewalk twice a day,
knew half the neighborhood by first name and odd need.
Those plate glass windows offer no such welcome,
Just faceless cashiers numb to the checkout stampede.
They say it's better, cleaner, brings in jobs,
But progress never smells like grandma's bread baking,
Or lingers for a chat over cracked checkerboards.
Each swipe of a credit card rings hollow as a knell.
A lost kid wanders past, backpack slung too low,
Eyes searching for familiar landmarks swept away.
They don't tell you in those economic forecasts,
How easy it is to misplace a soul on "upgrade" day.

45. pigeons on a power line

Squatters on a wire, oblivious to voltage,
a motley crew with puffed-up chests and beady eyes.
They bicker and strut with miniature grandeur,
gangsters of the urban skyline, feathers ruffled royalty.
One pecks at a discarded french fry, a stolen feast,
another bobs its head in what must pass for pigeon dance.
Their coos like garbled gossip, the secrets of the streets,
as farcical as the suited rush hour parade below.
They eye us humans with bored disdain,
knowing the city is truly theirs, no matter how we build.
Their droppings are graffiti against spotless windows,
a tiny rebellion against our notions of urban order.
Maybe these puffed-up birds ain't so dumb after all,
their perch above the chaos, a zen philosophy I miss.
A reminder that beneath the concrete and the rush,
life persists - feathery, defiant, and strangely content.

46. the bookstore owner

Spine-cracked paperbacks line his domain,
each faded cover a portal to whispered worlds.
Dust motes dance in sunbeams slanting through unread stacks,
the ghosts of countless stories waiting to be rediscovered.
No algorithm here to guide his weathered hand,
just a touch that recognizes a reader's hunger in their gaze.
The scent of old pages battles the latte shop next door,
a paper and ink war against the fleeting digital trend.
He's seen them come and go, these big-box behemoths,
flashing their discounts and soulless aisles as lures.
Yet, each creak of his floorboards is a victory,
each dog-eared page turned, a battle won.
A child lingers by the worn picture book shelf,
finger tracing worn illustrations, eyes lost in wonder.
Hope flickers in the old man's smile -
this is the fight he wages, word by quiet word.
Maybe his shelves won't always overflow,
the rent man always knocks a little louder each month.
But he is the caretaker of dreams, a quiet curator of the soul,
and that stubborn love shines brighter than any neon sign.

47. the bartender

He polishes glasses, wipes the worn mahogany,
a ritual before the symphony of sorrows begins.
Each slammed shot, a tiny explosion echoing larger ones,
celebrations and broken hearts swallowed back in unison.
His hands, a silent confessional to spilled secrets,
witness to first dates blooming awkward and love turned stale.
Laughter mingles with whispered deals and lonely desperation,
each clinking ice cube marking some unspoken struggle.
The suit at the end of the bar nurses a top-shelf single,
victory or ruin swirling in its amber depths.
The girl hunched over sugary cocktails hides tears,
mascara tracing heartbreak into the condensation rings.
They don't see the therapist in his crisp white apron,
how he reads despair in the angle of a jaw, triumph in a smile.
He pours another round, a liquid bandage for unspoken wounds,
offering quiet solace as neon flickers hide faded dreams.
When the bar finally empties, and dawn threatens his domain,
He scrubs away the residue of lives passed through.

His own reflection barely glimpsed in the polished bartop,
Just another weary warrior on the front lines of human need.

48. a graffiti

Underneath the rumble, past flickering fluorescents,
an underground gallery flashes unseen by most.
Spray can hisses like whispered rebellion,
defiant colors blooming on sterile, city walls.
Tags unfurl in swirling hues, cries of identity,
some crude, some intricate as forbidden tapestries.
Names painted bold, memorials to unseen lives,
or coded messages that only the initiated understand.
It's condemned as vandalism, eyesores to be scrubbed away,
yet under the grime, there's a raw pulse, a hunger to be seen.
In a city that prizes order, it's a middle finger to the bland,
a testament that creativity bleeds even in the underbelly.
Maybe it's just a name scrawled in the rush of passing trains,
or a haunting stencil demanding the world pay witness.
They'll wash it off, paint it over, routine as the morning rush,
but for a fleeting moment, art ambushed the ordinary.
A silent scream etched in paint on city veins,
this underbelly art won't win awards, won't grace galleries,
but for those who catch the flicker, there's a defiant beat,
a reminder that beneath the concrete, rebellion takes any
form it can.

49. trains

A monument to movement, the great station now lies bare,
Its iron veins exposed, the pulse of human tides withdrawn.
This symphony of farewells reduced to a desolate hum,
the loudspeaker coughs echoes into the vacant air.
They speak of plague, of fear keeping families far apart,
But this emptiness mocks those with no homes to flee to.
Where do migrant hands idle when trains cease to churn?
What hunger grows fiercer in this sudden sterile peace?
Those who swept dust now hold empty brooms, eyes bleak,
Each chai cup unsold tells a story of dwindling means.
This silence isn't caution, but the luxury of those with retreat,
Leaving those tethered here to navigate the void unseen.
A torn ticket flutters, a dream discarded on the tracks,
The timetable taunts those adrift in an unscheduled world.
Perhaps when trains roar back, they'll drown out these ghosts,
But for now, this emptiness exposes the fault lines within us all.

50. mob

They drag him out, a face twisted into a plea I can't hear,
just the roar of the crowd, a beast hungry for blood not its own.
The first rock flies, and something sick unfurls inside me,
not the righteous rage they whip up, but a trembling shame.
We were friends once, this one dragged and me,
shared stolen beedis, cricket dreams under the fading sun.
Now his skin's the wrong color, his faith the wrong shape,
and my hands clench with the stones they force upon me.
They yell of honor, of vengeance I barely understand.
Their words drown out the part of me that still hears him calling me bhai.
Maybe weakness keeps me here, fear of being outcast too,
a different kind of cowardice hiding in the angry surge.
The old banyan tree watches, the same one we swung from as kids.
Did its roots witness this cruelty before, these cycles we can't outrun?
I fling the stone, it clatters short, my aim skewed.
A tiny defiance, useless against the mob's terrible momentum.
They claim a victory when his body finally stills,
something broken beyond his flesh, in this land we all call

home.
Tonight, beneath the stars, I won't sleep, haunted by the look in his fading eyes,
and the part of me that died on that dusty road, beneath the weight of that stone.

www.ingramcontent.com/pod-product-compliance
Lightning Source LLC
La Vergne TN
LVHW040905150826
845672LV00007B/1898

* 9 7 9 8 8 9 2 7 7 4 6 9 7 *